Dreamsoak

DREAMSOAK
Will Russo

QUERENCIA

Querencia Press, LLC
Chicago, Illinois

QUERENCIA PRESS

© Copyright 2023
Will Russo

ISBN 978 1 959118 08 4

www.querenciapress.com

First Published in 2023

Querencia Press, LLC
Chicago IL

Printed & Bound in the United States of America

CONTENTS

Geraniums

Sunrise showed itself in. I wanted something
in my window box. Daylight

filling the lung of my living room, bathed
in a marigold breath. Someone keeps

closing the blinds. One day I'll strip them
off the frame. Imagine the atmosphere

another color, a kind of stained-glass planet
with air dyed a zaffer blue. Intelligent life, there's surely

more of it, asking what color it is
this morning, which sunbeams show

the fragile openings of a sanctuary. My flowers grow
tall as the tongue is bilingual. They need me

to water them. They need to be flirted with, light
courting soil, the way a wave washes the coast, stealing

until the sand is submerged. Seized, then released
a dried hostage. Low tide, the slow pour

of a sanguine wine, decanting. The window
keeping out a breeze. My trowel between fingers.

A day cools after so many hours.
I keep sprouting blisters, peeling off

blisters. Burst pads of skin like shriveled petals.
Why isn't the plural *gerania*? I took Latin.

As I deadhead, I smell
lavender. The sky ebbs toward something like it.

Darling, I'm Weary

Rain—L.A. bitches swear
it never happens. Out
the window screen I'm six
inches from, each gutter spills
a new highway, overture of a city
drowned in momentary
uselessness. I'm napping
by my solid man, the *sweep-flap*
of turned pages beneath
his slid finger. Thunder
augments cascade, serenade——Intermission,
him lifting my forearm to kiss
the lesion a street cactus pricked,
having parked too close to its curb.
Forgive my lagged body, beloved,
marked as a cardboard sleeve:
matcha latte with CBD oil. Alas———I'm asleep. I'm weary
of this branding. Everything I do
is expensive. May I please stop
doing? The smog pours inaccessible

       and this man with his pages
flicking like a left-turn signal. Nowadays
      —maybe it was always so—
I need music to stir, to wring the bulwark
of stiff joints. The strange movement
so long after holding.
What withdraws—
               is it conscious? When
               Alexa is summoned
               to wake, so am I. And
               that's called clout,
honey. And when she plays a song from a decade
I was alive for, the past only grows
longer, all time before now more
naive. To pilot this gift of myself———how could I fathom a thing
like forever?

You Sink You Glow

There does not exist a real intimacy that is repellent.
—Gaston Bachelard

What I do know: I want to write a home
around us, to breathe with sinewy young
lungs, unburdened by crust and tar, to do
the unspeakable things that make parents
grandparents. Alone, I lie
                   faceup, eyes closed,
    in voluntary dark, my brain heeding the still,
    the steady. Exhale. I can't decide what it is
I want, knowing less of you makes luxury—
the way one minute each day,
                   the sun goes earlier,
        toward winter. Sleep selfish; a weight
        (familiar at the fold of my neck) fulcrums.
        Pressed and lifted. Substrate in brief ink.
        I told my mother
                 I love men; she was the only mother
            to cry with joy. Do you see? I want always
            to show you something. How much I spring
            forward, you fall back. The sun is consistent,
            the planet's the problem. What have I gained
            besides an hour . . .

Drift

The wind kept blowing away
our footprints—where had we walked?

The edges of our unpaved road
wet to mud: the gentle borders of a scab.
They close in, fade, then flake to undergrowth.

We scatter bread for birds we imagine
will come like platelets clogging the wound.

Mountain ahead: slope and summit
skullcapped. Feet strapped—the forward,
downward ride.

We cave to what we tender.
An onion minced, broken down
and down again, digesting.

Our crumb trail
turning out necessary. Whatever
we snatch, call it a compass.
Whatever we spot, call its name.

Sky in Effigy

The horizons ring me like faggots
—Sylvia Plath

In any case, the story begins
with darkness.
—Cameron Awkward-Rich

A city this size, no one looks up, I'm illegible—

encircled as a little sun, scrunched up
on a windowsill. Smudge after smudge—

day strokes the dark, dwarfing night bottom-up.

Streetlights flicker
and fade, their light dies like all light.

A lit sky leaves debris
always on a water's body, a deep pool

of canal. Flowings with footbridges
bricking the difference.

Bikes chained to available iron.
Breath in the air as if pinned there.

A buoying houseboat appeals for address, man
juggles torches across the way. He draws

no crowd. My pen died writing this.

The canal sloshes through the mini-night
of a still-dark arch: the bridge

we skate-skated across—what does it share? Streets,
rails, blues, scaffolds, windows above?

We both once crossed it, meeting—nothing more. Were we
kids then? Was that youth?

Quick stall, traffic slows to bend
a vertex. This queer world, I speak its
language.

Buildings only so high—I steal an image
of sky. Now day acquiesces

to voyeur's evening. Men twice my age have called.

Lighter light melts from the water, warming
though never warm. The juggler sends

a final toss. Tip of my smoke burns
out. I'm in the husk of darkness.
Duskwind in the hair.

The moon withdrawn
behind nightcloud
makes no hazy difference.

Collection

The basement bedroom of my childhood
would flood. Sill-level, I saw my dad through aperture: rainwater
hemming his waist in the egress well. Each clog

he plunged. The well's only light, douse after douse, flickered,
finally, out. Surf jabbed the thin stiles of the window,
brimmed over our low shelves like a slow pitcher.

Dad kept two eyes on twelve horses at the track, grandpa drunk
and brooding over one son who wouldn't come—*know-nothing.*
Know-it-all. I couldn't blame him, wanting things whole.

I raced beads of rain against the car window, read books
with warped pages, pressed foam panels on my dad's studio wall.
His mouth held to the small cane of his sax, pipes

and valves shifted beneath his fingers. His breath bloomed
from the bell's open lip. Many times, I knocked too softly
at his door, spoke the low drone of complaint.

At church, he passed collection plates, palmed the broken lobes
of Communion, offering torn morsels of the body. If he split
anything for me and my brother to share, I wouldn't want it.

Promise

1.

The pond's icy surface—succumbing
to the wishes of opaque

and backlit clouds—has thawed. Frost
simmered and joined with dew.

I walk the murky bank, a ring lined
with wet cinders. Insects

remember hunger, prey
on the stalks of wilted cattails,
dousing their oils.

The high dock—there,
once white, now stained and sodden

on its perch. Spring, a muddy
promise, has been persuaded.

No one who saw me
yesterday will see me today. This
is who I've been—I've been wrong
to feel safe.

2.

      And the pond dislodges
from its cleft: contained and rippling, hard
as stone, ascendant. Fish scuttle within it.

Oblivious. As it lifts, it cuts the dock, which crumbles
to a cavern where all that has drowned
has drowned.

You Sink You Glow

Time enough   the breadth of bed

beside me lost your imprint   the moon ages in suspense

      enters the room in slatted light to filch

the dim affliction   I search the smoothed sheet

for hindsight   the sullied vacancy   my hand a weightless

      thing   we float

when we believe ourselves winged   strange how empty

you grow   I stretch

      linen's tension   it suits   dwells

less dense   this business of longing   of learning a body

      over again.

Legend

There was the War on Uncertainty. The country, curbed but unroofed in perpetual dusk. We walked the glass perimeter. Roots of trees poked from the ground like bent fingers. Highways stacked like rungs and held. I touched the small moon of your cuticle, the government of each knuckle. In the dream of this country, the body was a kind of wealth.

Winter summered to spring. Our snowcaps became headaches, our stomachs the engines of something unbreathing. Climbing your lattice left me filthy. My hands leveraged the window frame. This first threshold splintered, the next impossible—yet both had hinted at their frailty. The country was wide with greyblue leaves of rain. We wanted to stay.

Snake

I am cool
with the lights
out. Everything
is a modest
sun. My plumb
eyes, true and
colorblind,
zero brilliant
bodies. I do not
rule their color
or the color they
see. I shadow
warmth, seeing it.

Once

Once is the number of times someone loved me.
I saw my only love through window screens.

     I only saw my love. Through window screens,
     a noticing the way of others' bodies.

In noticing the ways of others, bodies
carried him into my waking life.

     I carried him in my awakened life
     and made a kind of theft in luring.

Luring, I made many kind thefts.
Wind would overwhelm my empty fingers.

     Wind—the emptiness that whelmed my fingers—
     withdrew, made of me a child when it left.

I was not a child when he left me.
Once is the number of times someone loved me.

Freddie

Sweet skinny boy
really put on
a show. Out of
Zanzibar, theatrics
took him steady
west—never could stop
his fleeing. Fluent,
flaunting hairless
shoulders, skintight
denim and torso, he
coaxed the tenor
of a virile genre—huge
jaw and extra teeth
open to a sky of
octaves. Frame a thin
sail. Boy could really
move those hips. Freddie—
all moustache and
fortune—you never sang
of men. How many
queens denied your
throat, your flung
voice? Whatever you
were, you weren't
just a fag, a shaking
vibrato, a ricochet
harmonizing solely
with itself—*and now I know*
             and now I know
             and now I know
             and now I know that you can hear me

Arithmetic

I couldn't tie my shoes. I thought
I'd never learn. My dad had said
as much. His legs stood twice
as high. We walked to school

together. I barely made it,
winters—roasting
in my wool, wind
chapping my cheeks.

That December when
my new coat wouldn't do,
I tore it from my body,
flustering my parents,

grandpa in hysterics. He loved me,
my mischief. Misunderstood
distress. We've both thrown
imperfection. I knew a googolplex

was greater than a million
but less than infinity.
Was there a number where
the naming stopped?

As some kind of lesson, my dad left me
at corners. I'd look up
in hope of him, lifted
as a digit out of sequence.

A Hurry

I grew up thinking
maturity meant losing

sleep. I did good things
to be remembered. Each

cigarette didn't taste
like the first. Love: infatuation

or a scene I streamed. I found women
difficult, men impossible—their blue

and white geometries. I had my whole life
for the good days amounting

to not-good weeks, our dead
who aren't watching us (not in the way

we think), and people with their precious genitals—
insufferable, everywhere. Every tree

with a fork clasped at the trunk, standing
guard, ready to strike. I quit smoking

the way a bed is made, the sheet thrown
like a flap of skin over what's puffy

and bare. I started thinking
in years. I don't beg

anymore. When I hold someone,
it's like I'm holding the only

thing. A body will force itself asleep
here in the city that takes its time.

You Sink You Glow

The dream in which you drown
gives me ground—lost as you are,

I seek and lonesome set out
down the shore. Ocean screws
a lid about your scalp. You are light,
and as you sink you glow

a bulb

               the water so bottomless
it becomes space, swarming with fishstars
sucking at oxygen. Is your body stored
in the vastness? Else, your picked-apart pieces
float—to where? Above, walking   walking

our distance grows: temporal, material, ardent—how am I to
measure? Of each other, we accept so little, so much.

Confession, in Andersonville

Oh dear, my sweet's got no potato.

Why can't I remember
a rain this heavy, this resistant
to what's to come?

Far north
of the freestanding city, I'm a whistler.
How can you people go on
loyally? Tweet tweet,

little bird I reflect in! It's payday
so I'll lose money slower. I can't wait
for tomorrow's coffee.

And it is raining onto mounds of snow.
I understand living as melting.

Stranger

I snuggled beside you in the last open nook
    on the train, the seated pair of us

        jostled herky-jerky, stop after zealous
    stop, until at once we were

    the only tandem two in the car,
        neither noticing the gradual relief

relinquished by the clearing of close bodies,
    and neither too needing to scooch

        or otherwise adjust our amenable formation,
    so we remained, entrusted

    to another, our outer thighs
        affixed—a Velcro not yet peeled apart.

Let Me Be

Last night, snow woke
the unfallen leaves with an early blow; this morning,
the groundskeeper takes a chainsaw
to the branches.

*

Dressing back to mirror, sponging
days-old film from the pan.

If I've been page, let me be
shelf; if shine, then rust
crawling a wet engine.

*

I'm not taking calls. A gust scuffs
my trimmed neck. Coffee drips
my fingers like wax. I can't help
ears from passing by.

*

Obvious
that everything borrows, for example—
flies: horse, dragon, butter.

The noseprint on my cup's lid.

*

When I want the thick sweat
of winter, I will have it
on my tongue. I will weave myself
in pliant blankets, gorge
until my belly pops.

*

It's important to stop
for a picture—to not walk through one
being taken by tourists. Orange slips
everywhere. Due to non-payment, gas supplying heat
will be disconnected.

*

If I am prostrate as a shadow, it is
of my own doing. When I stomp,

there'd better be earth
to bounce from.

*

Isn't it funny
you can't give yourself
a papercut if you try?
What I mean is,
there's no right way but plenty
of wrong.

*

If grass is milk
and honey, my faith is alley.

Let me be untouched as art.
I won't beg; I am worthy
of this want.

*

Let the bus pull away—let
me be nothing to it.

The weather has cooled.
It leads my slow turning.

Soldierfish

Glares I dodge
shine me silver;
behind glass, pebbles
piece this puzzle. Bright
waves. Light dives; I hide
but cannot burrow. I am
careful what to catch
in my bloated jaw,
the sunken petal
of each eye. Nets
scale the ocean
for flat red bodies
tilting like mine.

At Once Sealed and Soluble

after Charles Wright

Bedroom

A course of brickwork. Maze of mortar gluing head to head,
bed upon bed
                    stacked flat towards a sky on which I can't
lie. Wall's a cutup, sum of parts. Perfection of right angles

foreboding, forbidding oblongs and obtuses, acute vertices.
Add the corners, they make a circle—tessellations
of box spring, infinity mirror. I've said this before:

straightness is manmade. Rod and rhombus, lozenge, square—
they go round and round around
                              an axis. Planet ever-turning
its head away in shame.
                    Darkened into so many halves.

Tree Roots

Evergreen is bone and pigment. Grows projectile out of ground.
Boughs snapped for thick blood. Resin drains from once-limbs
like beads of paint—is this rumor? Gamboge: top-heavy with
   unripe fruit,

the tree bears the yellow name without resemblance:
                                   adopted child.
Did the gum once flow within the tree, or does this method
transplant stillness? Pollen-soaked hot spring

and smaller remedies. Over their bodies, monks fold robes—
the color of alchemy drips shoulder to ankle. Only
a name stitched, very small, in white thread.

Wheat Field

How yellow the room became, morning streaking in.
Your fingers on my jagged lines: thick bumps of paint,
as if a song in braille, and blood so dry it flakes.

You fit in my palm like the lightfast colors
                                        of spices, synthetic
tints squeezed from tubes. Our drunken, immortal orpiment
overtaking other yellows—cool oatmeal sheet to a coat of king's
    gold.

A field another mirror. An empty search. Even the sun
with its angles, the dipped tip of my arrow
flying, flows through the earth in its veins.

———————

Bedroom

Had a dream. A piano descending, its descent
                                        deliverance.
When my life is over, forget the shortcoming of my dramas.
The hourglass and its many acts. *Remember*

when we were together, the scene of scratches and scrolls
lining the walls in a sequence memorized
as a saved date. Fluids correctional
                            and textual. Remember the raw

opening of a tomb; seal mine with poisoned wax. It has awakened
against you. *We were alone and I was singing
this song to you*. Behold, it comes.

———————

The Poet

Chronic disease, overwork, sadness: the patience of a brother.
Where'd his letters go?
                    Overshadowed, flowers' need not met.

I painted your portrait—another box you fit in. The color
of your shirt and cheeks
                    the same. I said, "I am here
to paint infinity," and made each star a proud printed hoof.

Hair shed from a hide. Grandson,
                         murdered impresario.
Illness makes selfishness, giving all we have
                              to ourselves...

Worn Out

Every sport's a war. Clay court, balls of neon felt, the path
leading nowhere. Ball boys. *Be copy now*
                    to men of grosser blood.
Shame—conflicted of the dangers, being seen or being

caught. *Let us swear that you are worth*
your breeding. Secrets kept, waiting for me to find them hidden.
A jaw broken into as a vault, a fault not of steel but of what's
   to be stolen.

Wasp caught in a web, sticky tangle of wings; spider crawling home
to meet her feast. Combat
                    of spindly legs and stinger.
Such horrors. Only such horrors.

Bedroom

We were too young for Frank O'Hara—for too much coffee,
too many cigarettes. After sixty years, I still won't know
where to lie.
        In our anxious quarantine, a suicide sold—the hoax

of a priceless, violent relic: gun found by a man who fires
clay. Ceramic puzzle box, repetitious mosaic. The latch
loosens; pulled like a crush, the shackle splits

from its body. A lock is an impasse,
                    at once sealed and soluble.
Wheel, spun towards a sole code, that adorns what needs holding.

––––––––––––

Irises

Sky's a limp blue, cowering and covering the cloud tops.
Albedo, budget, shield, and filter. *Then lend the eye
a terrible aspect.* Whiplash, the drastic styles
                    of neighboring houses.

Stems cradle blooms—their tiny beards, flaps shriveling open.
Thread a picked one over a finger, heavy as betrothal.
                    *Now set
the teeth and stretch the nostril wide.* We're alone now. Sunset—

its red flames, bulk and monotone. A flattening.
Twin graves of devotion. Angle and outline.
Such asylums of the garden.

You Sink You Glow

I'm all dreamsoak and countermuscle. My holding body
holds. Is storage.

                            Little by little square,
tall by tall wall—each aframe with windows.

                                   How can I
trust what's hollow?   The sun come-hithers coy glass.

Once again I decide to pity you.

                           My stuffy apartment,
we'd float   thin kitchen to a fan's blown coil;

I'd lodge forearms
from your shoulders to skull and stretch you neckwise.

                   Box on box labeled Dishes, Bigger
Dishes; the wide panes   mocking our forms into one,

a borrowed shade behind us, my nose
to your cauliflower ear.

                       You were my clumsy world,
small rock I threw

                which broke, and the hardness grew
thatmuchfold.
Those small shames motionless.

A child, I heard my brother crying; I made sure

                            to hide
my joys.

        Clouds now.

                 Then the rain turns soft hail.

I'm no longer night's
beckoning road.   I'm glad I'm not.
                I can't handle another start.

To a Lover on Vacation

Because of our apple-sliced planet,
    it's tomorrow morning in Sydney,
where, to and from, you'll spend
    thirty planed hours in limbo, head

caught like floss between headrest
    and window, buckled in but mindful
of helplessness, the body's failures.
    There are many ways to count time,

I prefer to make it pass. Each time
    you leave, I clean the bathroom, take
to the vacuum. The sponge
    doesn't waste the faucet's gift, it cries

like most animals. I spray what makes
    grime vanish, shake out hair the bathmat
kept. The mirror won't hold
    one small thing back. I play dress-up, part

my hair on a new side. Thrust a brush
    to back pockets of mouth, wisdom holes
I prod once daily. The dentist tore gum,
    cracked molars into chips for the forceps.

I didn't mind the extraction—remedy
    concerns discomfort, your friend told me
of his own jaw and brain, where new
    tumors grew. I wished for remission

of distance, that healing
    wasn't reliant on touch
when what we do
    is reach. When you call, I listen

for what the phone can't patch: slouch,
    each dimple's gradient, friction of fingernails
between teeth. I know what it means
    to have what's hidden found. Still,

I love you still,
    in my hands cupped palm to cheek,
guiding you to my lips, the water
    digits sift on another shore. I haven't

changed the sheets, since making the bed
    was the last thing you did before you left.
I can't smoke in the summer, can't add
    heat to heat, but now afternoons brood

and I'm nearer to sleep. Whiff
    of the kitchen: coffee with mildew. Night shower
soaks and softens skin. Musty towels
    want to dry or be dry. We're mummified,

men swathed from two bruised
    boys. And your friend—weren't we anxious
for relief, any kind passing? Let your fingers
    graze my back, newly waxed, each pore pink

and opened. I am looking everywhere
    to be filled. I am I am (I am).

Motivated Forgetting

The station where a cop caught me one-legged
over a turnstile. My neighbor bitching
that I walk too loud. Restaurant
where I made a man cry, later foreclosed,
and the pavement cracked as a phone screen.
It all comes plainly

as the pinch of blood pooling
on my forehead. I've popped a zit.
It spat out everything it kept
hidden in a pore. I hadn't given
permission. It told me anyway
what I wanted.

Notes

The epigraph in "You Sink You Glow" is from Bachelard's *The Poetics of Space* (Penguin Classics, 2014. Copyright © 2014 by Richard Kearney).

The epigraphs in "Sky in Effigy" are from Plath's "Wuthering Heights" (*Crossing the Water* [Harper Perennial, 1980. Copyright © 1971 by Ted Hughes]) and Awkward-Rich's "Faggot Poetics" (*Sympathetic Little Monster* [Ricochet Editions, 2016. Copyright © 2016 by Cameron Awkward-Rich]).

"Freddie" borrows lyrics from "The Prophet's Song" on Queen's 1975 album *A Night at the Opera*.

"At Once Sealed and Soluble" is in conversation with the work of friend and poet Steven Hollander. The poem contains references to and borrows language from the titles of Vincent van Gogh paintings, William Shakespeare's *Henry V*, Franz Wright's poem "Roadside Grave: Winter, Mass," lyrics to Leon Russell's "A Song for You," Ezekiel 7:6, Theo van Gogh's official cause of death, and the discovery and auction of the gun believed to be used against Vincent van Gogh in 1890.

Acknowledgments

I extend my gratitude to the students and faculty of the workshops where these poems were drafted and revised—the School of the Art Institute of Chicago's MFA in Writing, the Kenyon Review Writers Workshop, and the Bread Loaf Writers' Conference. Specific thanks go to Janet Desaulniers, Tarfia Faizullah, Richie Hofmann, Nathan Hoks, Gabriel Ojeda-Sagué, Carl Phillips, and A. E. Stallings.

Earlier versions of these poems appeared in the following publications:

Cagibi: "Collection" (as "Saxophone")
Faultline: "Legend"
FEED: "You Sink You Glow [The dream in which you drown]"
MAYDAY: "At Once Sealed and Soluble"
Meniscus: "Drift"
Newtown Literary: "Geraniums," "Darling, I'm Weary" (as "Rain"), "To a Lover on Vacation"
Salamander: "Once"
SPECTRA Poets: "You Sink You Glow [Time enough]," "Freddie"
Watershed Review: "You Sink You Glow [What I do know]," "You Sink You Glow [I'm all dreamsoak]"

ABOUT THE AUTHOR

Photo credit: Yalie Kamara, ed. Alicia Prieto

Will Russo is a poet, editor, and drummer based in Chicago, Illinois. Born and raised in New York, he graduated from Brooklyn Technical High School before attending Emory University and finally the School of the Art Institute of Chicago, where he received his MFA. *Dreamsoak* is his first chapbook. Visit him at willrusso.com.

CPSIA information can be obtained
at www.ICGtesting.com
Printed in the USA
BVHW052102100323
660188BV00004B/6